10-Minute Crafts

ORIGAMI CRAFTS

ANNALEES LIM

WINDMILL BOOKS

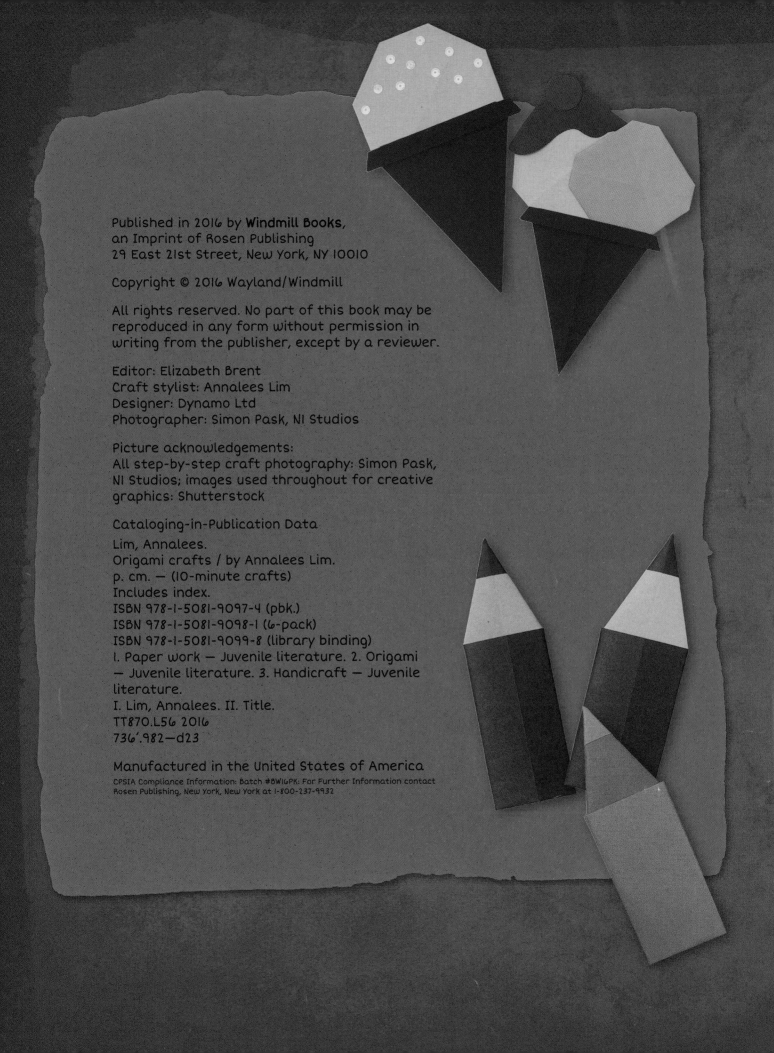

Published in 2016 by **Windmill Books**,
an Imprint of Rosen Publishing
29 East 21st Street, New York, NY 10010

Editor: Elizabeth Brent
Craft stylist: Annalees Lim
Designer: Dynamo Ltd
Photographer: Simon Pask, NI Studios

Picture acknowledgements:
All step-by-step craft photography: Simon Pask,
NI Studios; images used throughout for creative
graphics: Shutterstock

Cataloging-in-Publication Data
Lim, Annalees.
Origami crafts / by Annalees Lim.
p. cm. — (10-minute crafts)
Includes index.
ISBN 978-1-5081-9097-4 (pbk.)
ISBN 978-1-5081-9098-1 (6-pack)
ISBN 978-1-5081-9099-8 (library binding)
1. Paper work — Juvenile literature. 2. Origami
— Juvenile literature. 3. Handicraft — Juvenile
literature.
I. Lim, Annalees. II. Title.
TT870.L56 2016
736'.982—d23

Manufactured in the United States of America
CPSIA Compliance Information: Batch #BW16PK: For Further Information contact
Rosen Publishing, New York, New York at 1-800-237-9932

Contents

Origami

Origami is the ancient Japanese art of paper folding. The word comes from the Japanese words oru, which means "folding," and kami, meaning "paper." It usually uses square, colorful pieces of paper to create a whole range of 3D models, from animals and people to houses, cars, and much, much more. There are hundreds and hundreds of designs you can make – you will never get bored of origami!

The first instructions about how to make an origami crane were written in 1797, and the same technique is still being used today. An old Japanese legend says that if you fold one thousand cranes then you will be granted a wish. The smallest crane ever made was folded from a piece of paper measuring less than 0.004 square inch (0.3 sq cm), while the biggest measured more than 256 feet (78 m)!

In this book you will learn some basic paper-folding techniques to introduce you to the art of origami. The first step is to find something to fold. You can buy special origami paper in most art shops but there will be lots of things you can use from around the house, too. The best kind of paper to use is not too thick, so scrap pieces, magazine pages, newspapers, envelopes or even sheet music are perfect. If you do use paper that is not shop-bought, make sure you cut it into squares beforehand, though. Each side of your square should be about 6 inches (15 cm) long.

The projects in this book will let you transform a flat piece of paper into nine fun crafts. Some projects will make 2D shapes and some will make 3D shapes, but each one will take under 10 minutes to do. The most important thing to remember is when you make a fold, be sure to press down firmly to create a proper crease. This will make the rest of the steps easier.

This is not a messy craft and can be done anywhere, but sometimes you will need to draw on the paper before you start folding. Make sure that you cover any surfaces with a sheet of newspaper or a plastic sheet to protect them from pencil or pen marks when you are doing this.

A note about measurements
Measurements are given in U.S. form with metric in parentheses. The metric conversion is rounded to make it easier to measure.

Flower

This is a really simple flower to make. Once you have mastered it, try stapling lots of flowers around a ring of card stock to make a fancy wreath. You could also attach florist wire to the bottom of the flower and wrap it around a napkin to make a pretty table decoration.

1 Fold the piece of paper in half from corner to corner, and then in half again to make a triangle. Open it out.

2 Fold it in half and half again to make a small square, then open it out again.

Fold the paper in half to make a triangle. Fold the right point across to the left edge.

Turn the paper over and fold the right-hand point over to the left side.

Fold the right point in to meet the right-hand folded edge. Do the same to the left point. Fold the bottom point behind to make a flat base and curl the top edge over.

Finish the flower by gluing it to a colorful background and adding a green stalk and base to the bottom.

T-shirt

This is one of the only origami techniques that uses a rectangular piece of paper. Decorate the T-shirt to make your own fashion design, or to match the shirts of your favorite sports team.

You will need:

- A piece of paper, 4 by 6 inches (10 x 15 cm)
- A ruler
- Pens or pencils (optional)
- String and mini clothespins (optional)

1

Fold up the bottom of the paper by 4 inches (10 cm), turn it over and then fold it in half lengthwise and open it up. Fold each side into the middle fold.

2

Fold out the top of the right-hand rectangle to make a triangle. Do the same on the other side.

8

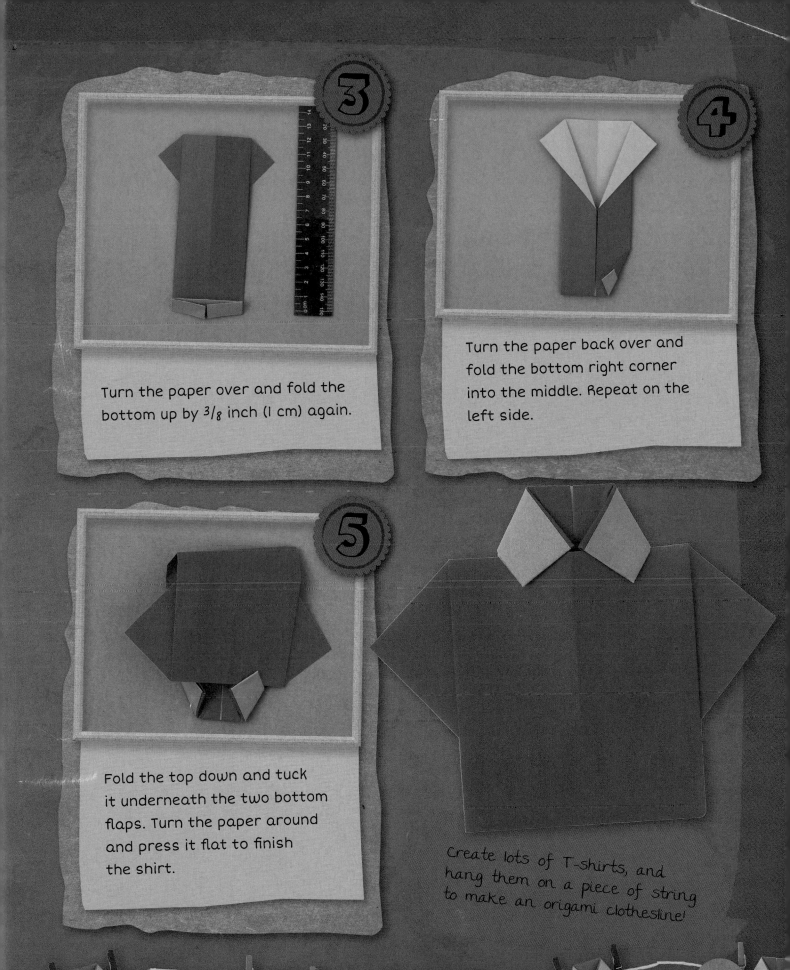

3

Turn the paper over and fold the bottom up by 3/8 inch (1 cm) again.

4

Turn the paper back over and fold the bottom right corner into the middle. Repeat on the left side.

5

Fold the top down and tuck it underneath the two bottom flaps. Turn the paper around and press it flat to finish the shirt.

Create lots of T-shirts, and hang them on a piece of string to make an origami clothesline!

Box

You can make this box using paper of any size. If you make a second box using a slightly bigger piece, you can turn it into a lid for your first box!

1

Fold the paper in half and half again to make a small triangle. Open this up and fold each corner into the middle.

2

Fold the bottom edge into the middle and do the same with the top. Unfold and do the same with the two side edges, then open up to see all of the square folds you have made.

Open up the two side edges and fold the top and bottom up to make the sides of the box.

Fold one of the sides up, making sure you tuck in the paper to make the corners.

Fold the top point down into the middle of the bottom of the box. Repeat steps 4 and 5 on the other side.

To turn the box into a house, make another box, and cut it in half to make a triangular roof. You'll have to tape it in place to stop it from falling apart

Puppy

You will be so proud of this paper pup, you'll be parading it around for all to see! Once you've mastered the technique, try making a whole litter of puppies with different-colored coats.

You will need:

- Brown origami paper
- A black pen
- Red paper
- Scissors
- A glue stick

1

Fold the paper in half, corner to corner, and then in half again to make a small triangle.

2

Open it out once, with the point of the triangle facing you. Fold down the right-hand point to make an ear. Repeat with the left-hand point.

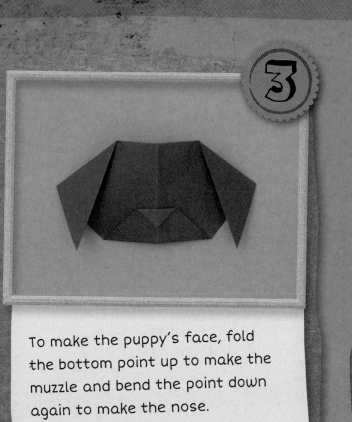

To make the puppy's face, fold the bottom point up to make the muzzle and bend the point down again to make the nose.

Fold the face in half slightly and press in the bottom to make a mouth.

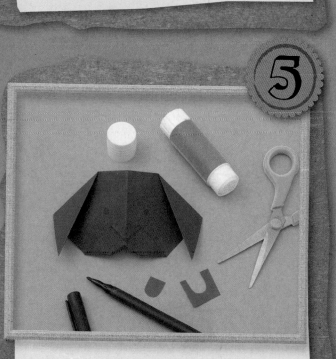

Use the black pen to draw on the eyes and nose. Cut out a red tongue and stick it in the mouth.

You can fold a piece of paper the same color into a triangle and glue it to the head to make the puppy's body!

Panda

Use double-sided paper, or color one side of a piece of white paper black before you start, to make this white bear transform into a panda!

You will need:

- origami paper, with one black side and one white side
- A black marker
- Adhesive tape or glue (optional)

1

Fold the paper in half, and half again to make a small triangle. Make sure no black is showing at this stage. Open it up to make a larger triangle, with the point facing towards you.

2

Fold the right-hand point into the middle fold, then fold the point back on itself so that it reaches the outside edge.

Press the tip down into a square and fold the bottom point up to reveal the black. Repeat steps 2 and 3 to make the other ear.

Shape the head by folding the corners back behind the ears.

Fold up the bottom point to make the mouth, bend down the tip to make the nose, and tuck the top down in behind it. Draw the eyes and mouth on with the marker.

You can make a body from another sheet of paper, about a quarter of the size. Fold over each corner to make the hands and feet, and stick it in place.

Cat

This is the cutest kitten around! Try making a scoop of ice cream from pages 22–23 and turning it into a ball of wool for your cat to play with.

1

Fold the paper in half into a triangle, and open it up so that the crease is horizontal. Fold the top point over to meet the middle.

2

Fold the paper over at the crease, then fold both top points down and in to meet the bottom point.

Bend each point up again to make the ears. Turn the paper over.

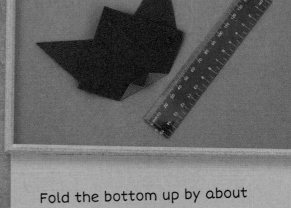

Fold the bottom up by about 3/4 inch (2 cm) to make the face, and then fold the point back down to make the nose.

5

Fold the top point down behind the face. Use the felt-tipped markers to add eyes and whiskers, and to color in the nose.

Make a body and a tail for your cat out of a small card stock triangle and a long, curly strip of card stock, and glue them in place.

Penguin

Paper penguins are like real penguins – they like to hang out in groups, so be sure to make two so your penguins aren't lonely.

You will need:

- origami paper in two different colors

1

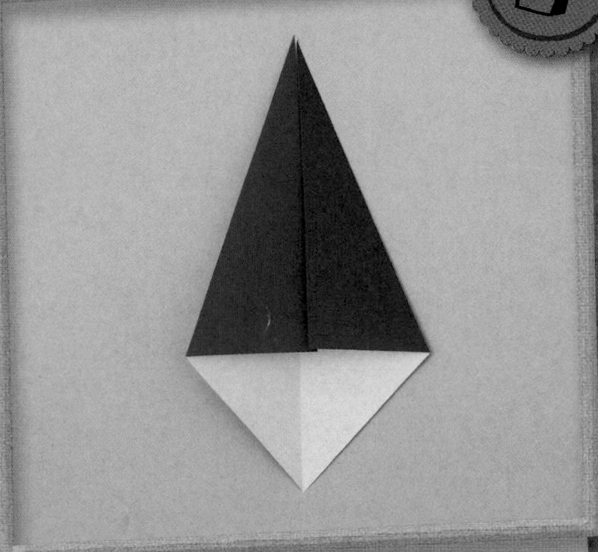

Fold the paper in half into a triangle. Open it out, and then fold each corner into the middle crease to make a diamond shape.

2

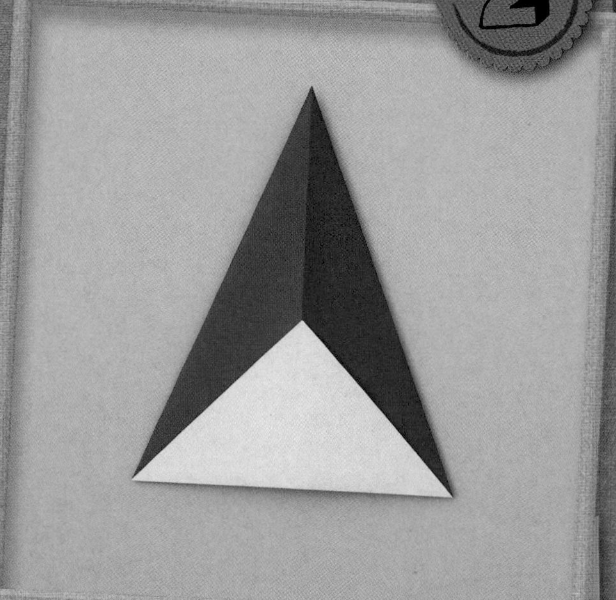

Turn this over and fold the bottom up to make a triangle shape. Turn the paper over again.

3

Fold the top down and bend the point back up to make the beak.

4

Fold the top down to form the head.

5

Fold each side out and back in on itself to form the wings.

Fold the penguin in the middle to make it stand up.

Coloring pencil

These pencils need to be made from a rectangular piece of paper that is brightly colored on one side and a paler color on the other side. If you have trouble finding this, you can always paint or color in a piece of paper.

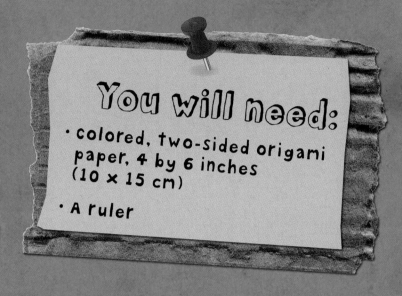

You will need:
- colored, two-sided origami paper, 4 by 6 inches (10 x 15 cm)
- A ruler

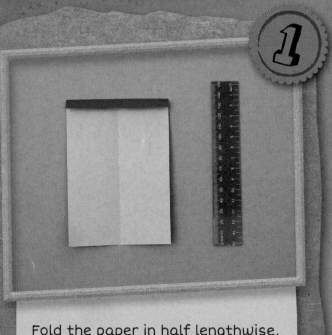

1

Fold the paper in half lengthwise, and then open it up. Fold the top down 3/8 inch (1 cm) and then turn the paper over.

2

Fold the top corners down in towards the middle crease.

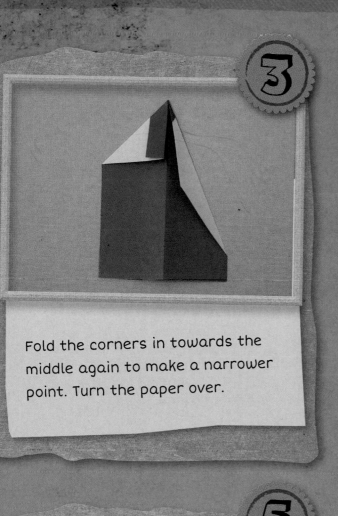

3

Fold the corners in towards the middle again to make a narrower point. Turn the paper over.

4

Fold the bottom edge of the paper up so that just the top point is showing.

5

Fold the sides back to finish the crayon.

You can make a whole set of coloring pencils in lots of different colors. They also make really great bookmarks!

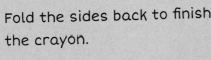

Ice cream cone

Summer is not summer without a delicious ice cream. The best thing about this one is that it won't melt!

1

Fold the orange paper in half into a triangle and open it up. Fold the left- and right-hand corners into the middle to make a diamond shape.

2

Fold the top point down, then turn the paper over. Fold the top edge down to make the top of the cone.

Make the ice cream by folding the yellow paper into quarters. Open it up, then fold the corners into the middle.

Fold in all four points, and turn the paper over.

Stick the ice cream into the cone, and stick some sequins onto the ice cream to decorate it.

One scoop isn't enough! Make lots more scoops of ice cream, sauce, or even a cherry to go on top!

Websites

For web resources related to the subject of this book, go to: www.windmillbooks.com/weblinks and select this book's title.

Glossary

crane a large bird with a long neck, which is a holy creature in Japan

florist wire metal wire used in the arranging of flowers

litter a group of puppies born to the same mother at the same time

sheet music musical notes written on pieces of paper

technique a way of doing something

wreath a ring-shaped garland of flowers

Index

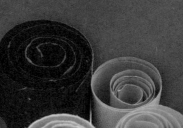